I work on a Building Site

by Clare Oliver

Photography by Chris Fairclough

W
FRANKLIN WATTS
LONDON • SYDNEY

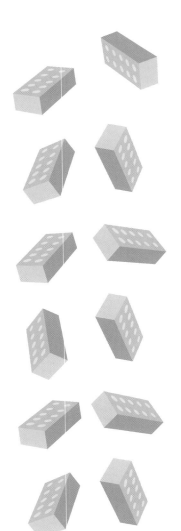

First published in 2001 by
Franklin Watts
96 Leonard Street
London
EC2A 4XD

Franklin Watts Australia
56 O'Riordan Street
Alexandria
NSW 2015

ISBN: 0 7496 4202 5
Dewey Decimal Classification 690
A CIP catalogue reference for this book is available
from the British Library

Printed in Malaysia

Editor: Kate Banham
Designer: Joelle Wheelwright
Art Direction: Jason Anscomb
Photography: Chris Fairclough
Consultant: Beverley Mathias, REACH
REACH is the National Advice Centre for Children with Reading
Difficulties. REACH can be contacted at California Country Park,
Nine Mile Ride, Finchampstead, Berkshire RG40 4HT. Check out
the website at reach-reading@demon.co.uk or email them at
reach@reach-reading.demon.co.uk.

Acknowledgements
The publishers would like to thank Rod Johnston, the
workers at Turkington Holdings, Belfast, and Valerie
Christie for their help in the production of this book.

Contents

(Note: words printed in **bold italics** are explained in the glossary.)

Meet Rod

The building trade is perfect for people who like being outdoors. Rod can't bear being stuck inside all day. He has worked on building sites ever since he left school. He began as a labourer, but now he drives the **forklift truck**.

Rod works for a building firm called Turkington Holdings. He goes wherever the firm sends him. At the moment, he is on a brand-new housing estate, but in a few months' time he might be working on a shopping centre or a huge office block.

Rod is 24 years old. He loves working outdoors.

This is the building site where Rod is working at the moment. It is a new housing development.

There are loads of different jobs on a building site. All of them require special skills and training on the job. Driving the forklift brings Rod into contact with all the different workers.

The forklift carries heavy objects around the site. This is a load of concrete windowsills.

When there isn't much to transport on his forklift, Rod helps the other labourers on the site.

Forklift Truck Driver

Rod's most important duties are:

- Transporting heavy loads
- Signing for deliveries of materials
- Putting new materials in the yard
- Helping out wherever he is needed

The Foundations

The estate that Rod is working on is divided into plots – one for each house. Before construction can begin, the plot must be level. A digger scoops away earth until the ground is roughly flat. Rod can't drive the digger yet, but hopes to pass his test soon.

Before work starts, Dermot, the *surveyor*, checks the *architect's* plans in the office with Alan, the site manager.

Next, the house's **foundations** must be dug out. The builders mark out where the foundations will be. First they use string and stakes, then Rod uses a spray gun to mark the outline. Now the digger has a guide.

Rod sprays yellow paint on the ground to mark where the foundation trenches must be dug out.

Essential Kit

These special tools ensure the ground is level:

- **Theodolite:** this mini-telescope's lens has cross hairs (like the sight on a rifle) which are used for checking angles.
- **Spirit level:** this is a long tube of glass with a bubble of air trapped inside it, which is mounted on a wooden or metal pole. When the bubble is central, the workers know that the spirit level is level.

Surveyor

Dermot is the site surveyor. His jobs include:

- **Reading the architect's plans**
- **Measuring out the plots**
- **Checking that the ground is level**
- *Supervising* **the concrete-pouring**

▲ Rod holds up the spirit level while Dermot looks through the theodolite to check that the trench is level.

The holes are filled with concrete the same day, before they cave in or fill up with rain. The concrete comes ready-mixed in a huge lorry. Using shovels, rakes and wooden **T-bars**, Rod and the other labourers pat the fast-drying concrete. This makes the surface rough and **furrowed** – all the better for sticking to **mortar** or other materials.

The foundations will dry out overnight. Then the brickies can start work. ▼

Bricks ...

Bricklaying is specialist work. Rod cannot lay bricks himself, but he certainly helps the bricklayers (or 'brickies'). All day he brings them **pallet**-loads of bricks and **breeze blocks**.

> Rod forklifts a pallet of breeze blocks to the top of the **scaffolding**. ▼

The red bricks make the outside (exterior) walls. The inside (interior) walls are built from breeze blocks – thick, concrete bricks. Between the exterior and interior walls, the brickies leave a gap for a layer of polystyrene. This **insulates** the house and keeps out the cold.

10

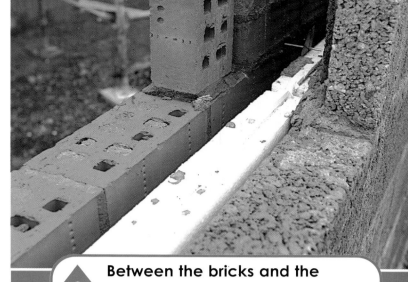

Another thing the brickies have to consider when they are working on the lower half of the house is the damp-course. This is a layer of waterproof material that stops the bricks soaking up water from the ground. It looks a bit like bin-liner material and nestles next to the polystyrene.

▲ Between the bricks and the breeze blocks, the brickies place sheets of polystyrene insulation.

Top Tips

Charley has been a brickie for more than 20 years. This is how he lays bricks:

- Spread on a bed of mortar with a *trowel* and flatten it to a thickness of about 2 cm.
- Squash some mortar on to the short end of a brick.
- Place the brick on the wall and tap it with the trowel handle.
- Repeat to the end of the row.
- Use a spirit level to check the row is even, and a *builder's square* to check the corners are true right angles.
- Repeat, but start the next row with a half brick.

▲ Charley lays a row of bricks for the outside wall. To give the wall strength, each row is staggered.

... and Mortar

Mortar is like gold dust on a building site. It really is the stuff that holds everything together! Like concrete, mortar comes ready-mixed on a lorry. It carries on mixing in the lorry, so that it doesn't set.

There is a fresh delivery of mortar every day or so. Rod prepares beforehand by lining the empty mortar tubs with plastic. When the lorry arrives, Rod helps the driver to channel the mortar down the chute into the tubs.

► Rod drags the empty mortar tubs to the place where the lorry parks.

► Rod helps the lorry driver to fill each of the plastic tubs with sloppy mortar.

MORTAR is a mixture of cement, sand and water. It is used to stick bricks together. It has to be used while it is fresh – before it sets hard!

Rod counts how many tubs have been filled with mortar, then signs the driver's delivery note.

When the tubs are full of mortar they are too heavy for anyone to move – except for Rod with his powerful forklift truck!

Rod then forklifts the tubs of mortar to where the brickies can reach them. The brickies take small amounts of mortar at a time. They carry it to where they are working on a **mortar board**, made from a small square of plastic or plywood.

13

Poles and Planks

When the brickies need to reach higher a team of scaffolders visit the site. The scaffolding poles and planks are quickly put together to make a climbing frame around the shell of the house.

Rod becomes a workhorse for a moment – carrying poles over to the house that is being scaffolded.

The scaffolders have worked as a team for years. Short shouts are enough to let each other know what they are doing.

Scaffolding is quite sturdy and safe – but it can still wobble a lot, especially when there are several people charging about on it. Like most labourers, Rod found this a bit alarming at first. Nowadays, he will happily walk about high up, even without any hands free for holding on!

The scaffolders are not employed by the building firm. They are a separate team from a different company. Their job is to turn up, **erect** the scaffolding as quickly as possible, and then move on to the next job. Scaffolders also supply very tall ladders. They paint these in their 'team' colours, so they remember to collect them when they come back to **disassemble** the scaffolding.

▲ Occasionally, Rod helps out if the site needs extra scaffolding and the scaffolders aren't there.

Tricky Moments

Scaffolders are absolutely fearless. They swing between the poles and climb up – even before the poles are joined together properly with the screw-down 'knuckles'. Walkway planks go down last, and are carried up ladders on the scaffolders' backs!

Rooftop Tasks

Once the walls have all been built, the roof can go on. Roofers nail felt and **battens** on to the rafters that form the framework of the roof. These come ready-made. Rafters and battens are too big to be lifted on a forklift. That's a job for the crane.

The roof is insulated with a thick layer of felt, which is nailed straight on to the rafters. Battens are then nailed on top of it. ▶

The roof tiles are stacked in a special way, so that they won't slip. ▼

The tiles are sent up to the roof on a special conveyor belt. They are stacked in tiny piles all over the roof, to make it easy for the roofers to work. It is important that the roofers don't have to move around too much carrying things, in case they lose their balance.

16

Chris is one of the roofers. He nails the roof tiles on to the battens.

Being a roofer isn't a job for anyone who is afraid of heights! It can be pretty scary looking down through the rafters at the concrete floor down below. But, like the scaffolders, roofers soon get used to this and develop an amazing sense of balance.

All the site machinery has to be checked regularly by Roy, the maintenance man.

Machine Maintenance Man

There's some serious equipment on a building site and it must be kept in good working order. A maintenance man's duties include:

- Driving to different building sites
- Checking cranes, conveyor belts, diggers and forklifts
- Fixing broken machinery
- Buying spare parts
- Keeping up-to-date with the latest technologies

Inside Jobs

Once the roof is on, the inside of the house is protected from the elements. The *joiner* fits the ceilings, using wooden joists and plasterboard. Rod brings him all the bits and pieces he needs in the forklift.

The houses are given a 'builders' finish'. This means the house buyer won't just get an empty shell.

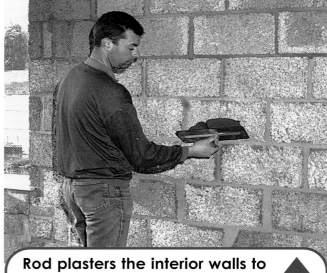

Rod plasters the interior walls to give them a smooth finish.

Plasterers apply a layer of smooth plaster over the bare breeze blocks. Rod sometimes helps with this, especially if it is too wet to work outdoors. The joiner fits wooden skirting boards, doors, stairs and banisters, while an electrician, or 'sparks', installs plug sockets and light fittings.

Brent, the electrician, is fitting a plug. Rod brings him a fresh reel of cable.

Finally, the decorators come in. They varnish the skirting boards and doors the way the customer wants them. And they tile the bathrooms with the tiles the customer has chosen.

Sean is the tiler. He has to kneel down a lot, so he wears cushioned knee-pads.

Martin smears grout all over the tiles, then wipes away the surplus. Grout stops dirt or damp getting into the gaps.

Top Tips

Sean has tiling down to a fine art:
- Check the plaster on the wall is dry
- With a trowel, cover the wall with adhesive
- With a spreader, make the adhesive surface rough
- Position the first tile
- Use pieces of card as tile spacers to keep the gaps between the tiles even
- Wipe the tiles clean with a cloth as you work
- Leave the tiles to dry. Next day, remove the spacers and fill the gaps with grout

Waterworks

From the very start of building a house, the workers have to allow for the plumbing. Pipes for the **sewage** are put in position even before the concrete flooring is poured in.

Even before any bricks go up, the sewage pipes for the house are all in place.

Once the roof is on and work has begun on the insides, the plumber arrives. Noel is the plumber for this site. He fits sinks, toilets, baths and boilers. He must connect the whole house to the mains water supply in the street, but of course he keeps the water supply off while he is working!

Rod carries plastic waste pipes around the site on his forklift.

Plumber

You need special training to be a plumber, but it's worth it. You will be your own boss and it is possible to earn lots of money if you work hard. You can become a plumber by studying for NVQs in Plumbing, up to Level 3. While you are studying, it is a good idea to take on a job as an assistant or apprentice to a plumber. That way, you will be gaining experience on the job.

Noel tightens the boiler washers with his spanner. If they are not tight, there could be a costly and dangerous leak.

Plumbing is complicated work. Noel installs a network of copper pipes that carry clean water from the mains, and a network of plastic pipes to carry away dirty water. Some of the clean water is routed through the boiler, so that it can be heated for the hot taps. Noel makes sure that the route for each pipe is as short as possible.

Noel has a special machine for bending copper pipes.

R od enjoys working on building sites for lots of reasons. At first, he just found it exciting to see how buildings were made. There was a lot to learn. When Rod buys his own house, he will know how to do most of the work on it by himself – and if not, he'll know someone who can lend a hand! Construction is a friendly business. Everyone helps everyone else to get the job done.

The workers on the site are a team – like one big, happy family!

There are people with many different skills on a building site. Jack has been a carpenter for over 30 years.

Rod chose construction so he could be outside, and to keep his body fit and athletic. He didn't want to be stuck inside a factory or a shop for his whole working life.

In the years he has been a builder, Rod has gained his forklift licence. Soon, he will be able to drive other machines, such as the digger and the crane. This sort of training is paid for by the company, but it makes Rod more skilled and means his wages increase.

Rod is proud of having passed his forklift test. He is the only forklift driver on this site.

Rod has another driving perk. He lives farther out than other people on the site, so he gets to look after the company van. He has to pick up fellow-workers on the way in each morning, but it means he can use the van at the weekend!

Rod is in charge of the company van, which means he doesn't have to buy his own car.

Being outside isn't as much fun in winter as it is in summer. Rod isn't vain but he knows that the wind and rain will batter his face and hands and make him look older than he really is. Some men on the site have problems such as **arthritis** or back pain. These come from years of stretching, lifting and being cold.

Some nights, when Rod gets home, he is completely worn out. That's because work usually starts as soon as it is light and goes on until it gets dark. In summer, that can mean working for up to 12 hours at a time. Sitting in the forklift isn't so bad, but there's lots of fetching and carrying to be done.

▲ **Rod has to do a lot of heavy work. He must lift properly and be careful not to hurt himself.**

Rod brings his own sandwiches. It can be hard to make friends on site, especially if Rod is just there for a day or two.

Although the workers all pull together, work on each site may only last for a few months. Then it is time to move on, and Rod has to get to know a new set of faces. Driving the forklift is more solitary than some of the other jobs. The brickies or scaffolders, for example, tend to move from site to site as a team.

Essential Kit

There is no uniform, but Rod has to protect himself from the weather – and from the dangers of the site.
He wears:

- Hard hat or safety helmet
- Old, hard-wearing clothes such as jeans and sweatshirts
- Brightly-coloured waterproof coat that is easy to spot against all the mud
- Steel-toed boots

When the weather is too bad to drive the forklift, Rod gets some grotty jobs – like sweeping the interiors clean.

The only **qualifications** for working on a building site are that, like Rod, you are strong, fit and hardworking. You have to love being outside and you have to be tough and resilient. If you complain a lot, or try to shirk work, the others will soon spot it.

You need to be able to pitch in as part of a team and also to show **initiative**. Rod tries to second-guess what job needs doing before he is asked, by keeping the brickies supplied with bricks and mortar, for example. That way, he doesn't hold anyone up.

These are the controls inside the forklift. Training to drive a truck like this happens on the job.

Rod is expected to show initiative. Without being asked, he hoses down the trailer wheels before they carry muck and dirt on to public roads.

26

Rod gets on well with his current boss, Alan. Alan is fair and looks after his workers.

Job Know-How

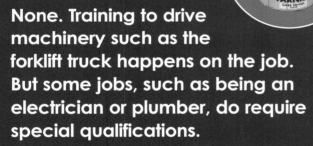

What qualifications do I need?

None. Training to drive machinery such as the forklift truck happens on the job. But some jobs, such as being an electrician or plumber, do require special qualifications.

What personal qualities do I need?

Strong, sociable, *punctual* and hard-working.

How do I apply?

Look out for job adverts in the local job centre, or apply through an employment agency that specialises in jobs in the building trade.

Will there be an interview?

Very rarely, but if you go through an agency the agency will interview you. Often, you are just expected to report to the site foreman at the beginning of the working day.

You cannot do **work experience** on a building site as it is too dangerous. However, you can gain experience by yourself by helping friends and relatives when they are working on their houses or gardens. Read DIY books for tips on just about every building site job, including bricklaying, tiling, plumbing, wiring and roofing.

DANGER
Construction
Site
KEEP
OUT

27

Glossary

Architect	A person who designs buildings, producing plans that the builders follow.
Arthritis	A condition that makes people's joints swollen and painful.
Battens	Planks of wood that roof tiles are fixed to.
Breeze blocks	Large, thick bricks made out of concrete.
Builder's square	Three lengths of wood joined together to make a right-angled triangle. This is used to check angles.
Disassemble	Take apart.
Erect	Build, put up.
Forklift truck	A truck with steel prongs in front that can transport heavy goods, especially on pallets.
Foundations	The base that a building stands on, usually made from concrete.
Furrowed	Describes a surface that has grooves or trenches.
Initiative	The ability to know what needs doing without being told.
Insulates	Keeps in heat and stops it from escaping.
Joiner	Carpenter.
Mortar	A mixture of cement, sand and water that is used to stick bricks together.
Mortar board	A square of plastic or plywood, used to carry small amounts of mortar.
Pallet	A wooden tray on which goods can be stacked.
Punctual	Arriving at the correct time.
Qualifications	Official requirements for a particular job.
Scaffolding	A framework of poles and planks that gives the builders platforms to stand on while they are working on a building.
Sewage	Watery household waste from sinks, toilets, washing machines, etc.
Supervising	Watching over other workers.
Surveyor	Someone who takes very accurate measurements to be sure of the basic structure and safety of a building.
T-bar	Two wooden sticks nailed together to make the shape of a letter 'T.' The bar is used to roughen the surface of concrete before it dries.
Trowel	A flat, triangular-shaped tool used to smooth on plaster or mortar.
Work experience	An unpaid period of work, often for a week, so that a person can see what a job is like at first-hand.

Find Out More

Write to the construction company that Rod works for:

Turkington Holdings
James Park, Mahon Road
Portadown, Co. Armagh

Visit these websites to find out more about construction in the United Kingdom.
www.building.co.uk
www.construction.co.uk
www.construction-uk.co.uk
www.careersinconstruction.com

Write to the House Builders' Federation for information about building regulations:

House Builders' Federation
56–64 Leonard Street
London EC2A 4JX

Visit the websites of specific construction companies to find out more about the work they do. Start with:
www.balfourbeatty.co.uk
www.beechwood.co.uk
www.bellway.co.uk
www.goldcresthomes.co.uk
www.kendrick.co.uk
www.laing-homes.co.uk
www.tilburydouglas.co.uk
www.westbury-homes.co.uk
www.wiggett.co.uk

There are NVQs that will give you extra qualifications for different building trades:
www.dfee.gov.uk/nvq

In Australia and New Zealand you can contact:
Construction Information Systems
This is a national directory of products and services. Check out their website at:
www.cis.asn.au

Other websites to look at are:
www.homeland.com.au
www.ausdesign.com.au

You can also find information from:
Master Builders' Association
(NZ) 0800-269119
Unitec Institute of Technology
www.unitec.ac.nz

Also, why don't you...
• Visit your local library and check out the careers section.
• Find out if there is a teacher at your school who is an expert careers advisor.
• Check in your local job centre and sign up with employment agencies that place workers on building sites.
• Look in your local business directory under 'Builders' to find out whom to contact for work experience placements.

Index